# Living Outside

## *the*

# BOX

*The*

*Goal Achievement Strategist's*

*Guide To*

*Reaching Your Full Potential*

**PATRICIA JO GROVER**

**Living Outside the Box,** *The Goal Achievement Strategist's Guide to Reaching Your Full Potential*

Paperback ISBN: 978-1-7350648-0-2

LOC: 2018963432

Printed in the United States of America

# DEDICATION

❧

To all my beloved grandchildren Landon Benjamin, Ryan, and Maisie Acosta. GG wants to make the world a better place for all of you, so this is my attempt to do just that. Hoping to make a positive difference for generations to come. I hope this legacy I leave you all will spark a passion for you each to leave legacies of your own! **XOXOXO**, GG

*Life is not really a problem to be solved as it is a mystery to lived!*

*I choose to live mine Purposefully, Joyfully, and Gratefully!*

*Patricia (Patti) Jo Grover*

# CONTENTS

𝓮𝓫

Only eight percent of people achieve their yearly goals. Learn about the software you were born with and how to conquer fear.

Set no more than three goals, dream big, and take the first steps of your journey.

# NOTE TO THE READER

౿

It is recommended that you read through this book completely before you try to begin using it as the tool that it was designed to be. Before you start doing the assignments at the end of the chapters, and applying the steps, you'll need a few things. The first is an imagination and a sense of adventure because that's what life is all about. You'll also need curiosity, courage, and consistency. These are important for having the right mindset when achieving your goals.

Other material includes:

- A one-inch, 3-ring binder with a viewing sleeve on the front and back. A one-inch binder space to work with per goal. This will be used for your goal sheets. If you're working on three goals, you'll need a three-inch, 3 ring binder.

- Divider tabs

- Notebook Paper (3-hole punched)

- Sheet protectors

- A couple of pencils

- Planner or calendar (I provide the "Design Your Destiny Planning System" FREE to all who join my Peer-to-Peer Mentoring & Accountability Membership Program, Peer-to-Peer Achievers Community, or my Empowerment Network & Mastermind Group. It can be purchased by those who would like to use it, but do not choose to become a member of any of my programs.) I recommend that you get a One Inch 3 Ring Binder to house the pages of your "Design Your Destiny Planning System." Before I designed this planning system to work along with this book, I have used a free version of Asana.com for business and personal projects. Find one that suits your personality and skill level. It can be digital or paper.

- To do this system using the least amount of paper I have two recommendations:

- First, Microsoft OneNote for Windows, where you can think with ink. Your notebooks never run out of paper. They are easy to organize, print, and share. Can do speech to text and even handwriting to text. You can access it from your smart phone, laptop/tablet, or desktop.

- Second, things like the NEWYES or Rocketbook are notebooks and calendars that have reusable sheets, calendar pages and QR Codes that you take a pic with your smart phone, it scans what you have written, and then instantly blasts your notes to your favorite cloud destinations. They are both great tools to have if you don't have your computer or smart phone handy, or if you are somewhere it would be considered rude to be on your phone. These tools can help you to keep your 3-ring binder in a digital version rather than a paper one. Some people find it easier to be able to carry their reusable notebook / planner and their smart phone around with them rather than a physical 3-ring binder. If you choose to build your 3-ring binder digitally, I recommend using One Note as a place to house your NOTES / ETC to keep them organized. There are several other options available to keep you organized!

Throughout this book, I'll refer to your 3-ring binder. The purpose of this binder is to build the foundation for your goals/dreams. It will be used for tracking your progress and as a quick reference for keeping your inspiration and motivation going. Long after you've finished this book (or have participated in any of my trainings, webinars, workshops, courses, or events) you can keep coming back to your binder and use it for new goals/dreams.

It will also include your Thought Starters, your Mantra, the Journey Elephant exercises, all other information that you will accumulate, and the Parking Lot exercise. These will be thoroughly explained later in the book and are available for download at www.patriciajogrover.com.

Once you get your binder(s) and other material, we can start to put the pieces of your puzzle together!

First, let's build your binder foundation.

## Build Your Binder Foundation

This is the most important step in the process of *Living Outside the Box,* you need to commit to yourself that you are going to do all the assignments I have laid out for you. This will require you to be digging deep within yourself, it may feel painful, and never ending, but I assure you it will all be well worth it! At the end of each chapter will be your Binder Assignments, where you will have to look deep within yourself, get real, be honest, and make the change or changes you need to reach the goal you're after. In your binder you will create various lists, build your WHY, hone your sensory vision, complete thought-provoking exercises, and ultimately be able to solve the jigsaw puzzle that is your life.

This binder will become your go-to source every time you have a new goal. It can be changed, added to, deleted, and used time and time again. *Each time you write in your binder make sure you date it.* This will show you the progression of your growth, which is important as you head toward your goal(s) and dream(s). Note that you will find dating each time you make an entry with be beneficial when you start putting you Actionable Plan together using your "Design Your Destiny Planner".

The front of your binder (the clear sleeve) is designated for a picture or collage of your WHY of the current goal(s) you are working on. The back cover (clear sleeve) will be for your mantra. These are necessary as you will want to view your goal(s) as well as review your mantra, saying it to yourself daily and at times aloud. We'll touch on the importance of these later.

Create a section for each goal. Each section will be kept separate and use its own corresponding tab.

Open your divider tabs and label them the following for each section (goal):

- WHY

- Fear List

- Graveyard

- Toolbox

- Obstacle List

- Need-to List

- Planner or Calendar

- *Parking Lot

- Notes

To get started putting your 3 Ring Binder together after each tab, insert one page of lined paper, except for the Need-to List, which will require four sheets. Toolbox and Graveyard will each need three sheets. Go to your WHY tab and at the top of the paper write WHY in capital letters across the top. Do the same for Fear List, Obstacles List, and Parking Lot. Next, go to your Need-to List tab and label the first page Learn, the second page Believe, the third page Have, and the fourth page Do. Under Toolbox, label the first sheet
Strengths, the second Opportunities, and the third My Other Findings. Under Graveyard, label the first sheet Weaknesses, the second Threats, and the third My Other Findings.

Under your Planner or Calendar tab, start making notes of things you will have to enter into your planner / calendar as you are thinking of them. Then go back to this section to make sure that you have gotten things entered into your planner and onto your calendar for tracking purposes. Make sure you have plenty of 3-hole punched paper for your Notes & Calendar tabs. This is where your Actionable Plan will begin to take shape. As you go through the various assignments, more paper can be added, as necessary.

Visit www.PatriciaJoGrover.com and print out six copies of the Journey Elephant (two for each section, One Elephant A and One Elephant B) and insert them between the Parking Lot and Notes sections, you will need these to refer to and make notes on. Also print out the Who Am I page and insert it in the sleeve on the back of the binder. We'll fill it in a bit later, as part of your Mantra.

As you use your binder, I highly recommend doing it all in pencil if you are opting to go with a physical binder, as your thoughts, ideas, and challenges will change as you move forward. Also, using the sheet protectors will give a longer life to each important page you've worked on.

Here I'm going to recommend getting a separate One-Inch 3 Ring Binder to house your "Design Your Destiny Planning System" that I have designed to work along with this book as you utilize what you are accumulating for information, start the habit of having planning days, start a tracking system, and be able to start plugging in some of the things from your Planning /

Calendaring Tab. It will be used when you begin to use the S.M.A.R.T.E.R. plan, but it can also be used in your personal life.

*The Parking Lot- is where you will put something that comes up until you are ready to move forward with that piece of the puzzle. Date every thing you put in there, and check to see what you have sitting in the Parking Lot every planning day!

The time is now to put your puzzle together!

# FORWARD

ॐ

## LIVING OUTSIDE THE BOX

Living Outside the Box, by author Patricia (Patti) Jo Grover, is well worth the read if you have a desire to:

- get to know yourself a bit better,

- get your life on track, and/or

\-      keep it on track as you move forward.

It was Albert Einstein who once said, "We cannot solve our problems with the same thinking we used when we created them." Patti Jo is inviting the reader to do more than simply think outside the box, she asks you to consider living outside this limiting cubicle.

The book not only offers suggestions and advice in that regard, it provides proven exercises and activities designed to facilitate the process of liberating you to the extent that you can continue both your personal and professional growth. I am honored to know the author herself has developed these steps as she worked over, around and through the obstacles she encountered in her life. I especially love the ease and flow of the chapters as they reveal each step.

Living outside the box is not only an idea whose time has come, by sharing her life experiences, the author is able to provide a mind-map that makes the journey easier and infinitely more enjoyable.

\-      Dr. Pauline Crawford-Omps

Author, Speaker & Gender Dynamics Intelligence© Creator/Expert

www.corporateheartinternational.com

First, thank you. Not for purchasing this book, but for taking the first step in a commitment to change your life and succeed at achieving your goals. I have spent my entire life as a student of it. Many of my lessons were learned through trial and error, but I take great pride in being able to say, "At least I tried!"

What made me finally write this book was I wanted to find a way to pass on all the knowledge and wisdom that I have accumulated over the years to my own grandchildren, and to others that may be looking for a system that provides the guidance and support that I've designed this book and my entire platform to be. Most parents want to give their children guidance to keep them from having to learn things the hard way. We would really like to help keep them from taking the long way around, to get to where they really want or need to be.

What also led me to write this book as the tool I've designed it to be is that my mission is to help as many people as possible to be Living Outside the Box that they may have put themselves in or allowed someone else to put them in. Really thinking back at the lack of education and support that my own mother had, and the years that I spent struggling, I wanted to be able to find a way to help primarily single women cut out better lives for themselves and their children. To break the cycles of Limiting Beliefs.

In my many years of struggles, I have grown. I have learned with errors also come losses, from losses comes pain, and from pain comes wisdom. Some of these lessons, losses, and pain have come from personal experiences self-inflicted by bad choices, sometimes from other people's bad choices, or just from how life happens. The rest of my knowledge and wisdom has come from reaching out to gain guidance and experience through reading books, attending courses, and hiring coaches or mentors.

I have benefitted over the years from other people's wisdom, been inspired with it, and it has motivated me. But it has also made me realize that most of these people that I had been learning from had been men. I also realized that if it were ever going to be any different for women, or anyone else in the future that I needed to find a way to change things up to be able to come across more nurturing and less matter of fact.

It has been proven many times over the years in studies that systems permit ordinary people to achieve extraordinary results. With this book and my entire platform, I have taken all the life changing information that I have acquired from other people's wisdom and arranged it into a format that makes it easier to utilize in today's world, broke it down to be able to be more readily recognized for its benefits, and simplified the process into steps by adding assignments.

So, what exactly is a system? My definition of a "System" is the process of predictably achieving a goal based on a logical and specific set of how-to-principles, utilized in specific sequences.

Something else that I have learned from other people's wisdom is "Don't expect someone else to believe something that you don't believe yourself."

One of the things that I learned when I was researching what it is that the 8% of the people that are the Achiever's do is that they all agreed that luck has nothing to do with success. It all boils down to finding the "SYSTEM", learning it, applying it, having the courage to do the hard work, and the consistency to stay at it until they achieved success.

A second thing that I learned when studying and researching those 8% was what huge effects that our beliefs and attitudes have on our possibility to achieve anything and have success. So much of what I share in my books and entire platform focus on these things.

I have some great news you: Given that you are reading these words right now you already have the necessary belief that you have a dream or goal somewhere inside you that you want to achieve!

I have learned that the best way to learn something the first step is to internalize it and make it truly a part of you enough, so it is easier to teach to others. Second, true joy and fulfilment come from giving, and from making a difference in the lives of others. This is simply the only real legacy we leave when our time here on earth is over.

In the case of good books, the point is not to see how many of them that you can get through, but how many can get through to you. --- Mortimer Adler, How to Read a Book.

Successful people do it now. They know that otherwise, they could fall victim to "The Law of Diminishing Intent," which states:

The longer you wait to do something you know that you should do now; the greater the chances are that you'll never actually do it.

In other words, what is the most important is that you take the initial step. Begin Now!

Don't promise yourself, "Well, I'll begin tomorrow", Tomorrow never comes: It always turns into today—and you didn't promise to begin "today", you promised to begin tomorrow."!

The good news is this action doesn't have to be perfect; it just has to be something. Naturally, the better you learn and more closely you stick to the THE SYSTEM, the quicker you'll achieve the results that you desire—but practically any action is better than no action at all.

Now that you have found a system that has been prove and will work for you, it is imperative that you apply it right away! So many times, people sit on their newfound knowledge, waiting for the time to be "just right" to utilize it. My friend, please do not do that to yourself.

You see, without applying your new knowledge toward a certain end, absolutely nothing will happen.

In order to move forward towards achievement of your goals and to have the life that you desire it's imperative that you act upon your new knowledge!

One of the only reasons that I have ever been able to come up with that people when they have that desire of achieving a goal and have found the system to aid them in achievement of that goal delay getting started is, FEAR!

What if's, and Buts. "What if it doesn't work?" Then I will really be a laughing stalk. "But, if I don't try, at least I won't have to go through all that disappointment of realizing that I couldn't do it." Or "What if it goes over so well and I'm not only able to help make changes in other people's lives to the positive, but I end up making changes in my own life that may be too big and scary."

Following this type of logic could have stopped me in my tracks, but I would have become so disappointed in myself for not trying, even more disappointed than if I had tried and failed, staying in that mindset I would have had no chance of success, and no chance of being able to help people worldwide.

This shows me that attitude is more important than facts. A person with a negative attitude may say "Here is the hard-tough fact of _____, you just can't get around it, a fact is a fact, and that is that." Where as a person with a positive attitude on the other hand says... "____, might be a fact but there are other ways to deal with this fact, such as go around it, over it, or hit it straight on and break it down so it can be no longer an issue."

A problem is only a problem if you cannot find a way to or do not take the time or make the effort to solve it!

I've found over the years it's best to think first before you react, I have had a saying that it's better to be proactive rather than to be reactive. Some people find it difficult to be a thinker, so I want to open your eyes to the different types of thinker that you can become.

One can become an "If Thinker" with all the What Ifs, or "If Only" OR you can become a "How Thinker" who immediately starts looking for solutions and wastes no time or energy on the negatives that stand in the way to achievement. How Thinkers are creative with their hows!

I had a childhood that would be hard for most people to conceive, let alone believe. As an adult I have experienced much pain and loss and have continued to overcome all those obstacles and come out better for it. This book is not written to be my memoir, nor is it written to say woe is me. On the contrary I'm sharing this info with you know so that you realize that I too am human, and if I was able to come from what I did, and been able to what I've done, and have the life that I have now, SO CAN YOU!

I will someday actually write that memoir, but until then I'll share pieces with you that may be able to help you as you are on your own life's journey. You find some of these pieces throughout the book and some in the About the Author section.

Perhaps my biggest lesson about the importance of how we choose to live our lives was in 2010. My husband and I were about to launch a new business in Florida when we were in a motorcycle accident. I don't remember getting on the bike that day or the accident itself. I have no memory of the ambulance, being airlifted on Life Flight, spending a week in intensive care, or coming home from the hospital. My injuries were a fractured skull, brain bleed, a completely blown-out right eardrum, and a torn rotator cuff. My recovery required enduring months of therapy—speech, physical, and occupational. After that, I suffered panic attacks just being a passenger in a vehicle, so I made two decisions.

The first decision was for us to get back on our motorcycle. During the first part of my recovery, I thought I'd never be able drive again and would have severe problems with my brain injury, but I'm blessed to be alive, walking, talking, with only a slight hearing impairment, and able to drive an automobile.

My second decision to come from all of this was to come back from the injuries (physical and mental) and be the best I can be. I've always heard the expression that life is short, and now I live that truth on a daily basis. Not long after my recovery, we decided to live one of our dreams, it was to own and operated a campground. We purchased a KOA (Kampground of America) franchise, grew it exceptionally for seven years, and then sold it. After selling the campground and now having much more time on my hands I choose to start living, planning, setting goals, and following dreams that I had for many years. Which was to write this book and create a platform that would allow me to help as many people as possible learn how to be Living Outside the Box, Breaking the Cycles of Limiting Beliefs, and to Design their Destiny.

Looking back on my lessons and experiences has inspired me to design a system which has worked for me time and time again. Now I've broken it all down into this book.

My writings, courses, workshops, and speeches are tied to this basic concept. There is such a great need for a system to be available for people who may not have been exposed to the fact that they can dare to dream, that they have the option to become what they want, and if there is a will, there is a way. There is a difference between easy and simply basic, which you will gain a better understanding of by reading this book and applying the steps of putting your puzzle together. Most times just breaking things down to the smallest pieces seems daunting, but actually makes it easier to comprehend.

It is said that the Lord/Infinite Intelligence has our lives planned out for us before we are born and represents our puzzle pieces and what the end picture will look like.

First, I'll share my philosophy of live so you will see how I have been able to bring this together to share.

When we are born, we are supposed to have at least one parental figure/guardian who is there to comfort, care for, aid, and guide us through our life. This person or people are also the ones that share or expose us to their Belief Window (s), before we are able to have a Belief Window of our own. It may not be the same person throughout our life and at times we may wonder who s/he even is. This person may not even be a blood relative. When we take our first breath, that is when we start putting together our life puzzle.

All our puzzle pieces at this time have been dumped out onto a table, which I refer to as "Life's Canvas." This is the point in your life when you literally begin *Living Outside the Box*. The puzzle pieces from our box are not the same size, shape, or color. There is no picture on the outside of the box, so we don't know what it is supposed to look like once completed. It doesn't even have the number count of how many pieces the box should contain.

After dumping the pieces out, some will land with the cardboard backing showing, while some are right side up with part of the picture showing. It is up to our designated adult(s) to start turning over our puzzle pieces to the side that starts to show us a picture of what our life will be. From that point, they start to separate the pieces which create the border/framework for our life. It is the duty of our trusted adult(s), until we reach a certain age, to keep all the pieces on our table. They become the keeper of the pieces, keeping them from getting eaten, falling to the floor, or becoming lost or stolen. In fact, they are supposed to be building our framework and introducing us to the interesting pieces that fit into place as our lives unfold.

Soon we reach an age when we are able to handle the pieces ourselves. We have gained enough experience to be responsible and help group pieces together by color. Our guiding person is still there and encourages us each time we try. His or her main objective is to keep all our pieces intact. At this same point in our lives we are only starting to see through our own Belief Window.

Then, as we get a little older and show interest in ourselves and how the pieces fit together, we start to realize that when the right colors and shapes come together it is kind of fun to see what we are creating in front of us. Our Belief Window begins to take on its own view.

As we continue to age, our adult is supposed to continue to keep our puzzle pieces from falling off the table. Should the pieces approach the edge and teeter, our adult slides them back to safety. However, if one should fall, our adult is there to pick it up and help decide where to place it on our life's canvas. Our Belief Window may begin to start showing us a new viewpoint.

Once we become young adults it's time for our adult to take a step back. S/he should no longer be the keeper and protect pieces from falling. However, s/he should stay close enough to help out should one fall or get temporarily misplaced. At this point in our lives the view that we may have out our Belief Window may still be remarkably like that of our adult. But yet may be taking on a different view that may make us start to ask questions.

By this time, we will come to realize that we cannot work consistently on our puzzle. This is due to many things happening around us, otherwise known as LIFE. It happens whether we are present for it or not. In the long term, this will be our friend. We will have a special or safe spot where we choose to store our puzzle. This way it will always be there when we either want or need to work on it. The important thing is always to schedule time to specifically go there and work on it. Now, not only is it our responsibility to manage our own puzzle pieces (life), but also our own beliefs as we develop our own Belief Windows.

There is always a breath of freshness that comes over you when you go back to that special place to look at where you are in your process/journey. It's quite a feat to see what you have compiled and completed since you didn't even have a picture to go by!

The time away from working on our puzzle is not always the same. Some of us are consistent for periods at a time, then go for years not even giving a thought to where we left off. Others end up coming to a point in their lives where they no longer want to continue to fly by the seat of their pants with no framework/background. There are still others who will be forced to find a way to get back to that place. Either way, it ends up being the best thing.

_**This is the importance of your binder. It is a safe place to track your progress and works as a reminder of why you're doing what you're doing.**_

As we progress through each chapter you will be filling in pages in each section tab. It also acts as a way for you to track your progress! Refer to your binder as often as you feel necessary. Some people spend time reviewing the binder daily, others weekly or monthly. Create a schedule that works for you and be consistent. *Those the most serious about achievement of their goals will work on it daily and learn the habits needed to work their plans of achievement.*

As we age, we sometimes find that the adults who were supposed to be there for us were not actually qualified for the position and started us off with a Belief Window that was not healthy in one or more ways. Once we realize that they have either intentionally or inherently guided us in the wrong direction, it then becomes our job to find a way to reach out for help and get a mentor. Sometimes as an unfortunate outcome of having a childhood where we did not have the right adult(s) for the job, we may have had one or more of our puzzle pieces lost, misplaced, or stolen.

If this has happened, it is up to you to take control and determine what your completed picture will end up looking like doing so by choosing to look out the Belief Window that you have created yourself. Just because it was made harder for you does not mean that you can't have full control of the end product.

*Life is not really a problem to be solved as much as it is a mystery to be lived! Our puzzle picture may in fact not just be one picture; it can be a collage of many stops on the journey.*

Go for it! You never know what may happen next. If not now, when? Be full of hopes about your future. Create a hunger to open doors to knowledge, direction, and achievement. Do it now, because today will be your yesterday tomorrow!

Life's biggest mistake is thinking that your life belongs to someone else!

I for one know that I want to leave this earth having as few Could Have, Should Have, or Would Haves as possible. Do you want to live your life and be able to say you never wished that you Could Have, Should Have, or Would Have?

I've taken my life experiences and learning and rolled them into a tailored format for the content of this book and my entire platform. At the root is a simple foundation that anyone can build upon to achieve his or her own dreams and goals.

I was greatly inspired by Lauren Catuzzi's book, *You Can Do It!* I took that inspiration and created a program that is appealing and helpful to everyone. I did not want to focus only on women but wanted to reach out to middle school aged children up to senior citizens.

What has really moved me to finally write this book is I'm now a grandmother of three amazing little ones, Landon, Ryan, and Maisie. I would like to leave a legacy for them which is this book and the entire platform I'm creating around it. My hope is to change this world for the better, for them and future generations.

What I mean by changing the world for better is empowering individuals to have better self- esteem / self - confidence so they are able to make better choices and decisions that will affect their lives in the most positive way possible. Because it ultimately is our Choices & Decisions that Design our Destiny. I want to teach people how to dream or even learn how to allow themselves to dream and to do so with Sensory Vision. Once they have the Dream down, I want to help them learn how to create S.M.A.R.T.E.R. plans, how to work those plans, and how to Achieve their Dreams & Goals!

I'm excited to announce that as **"Living Outside the Box,** *The Goal Achievement Strategist's Guide to Reaching Your Full Potential"* (which is the second edition of Living Outside the Box, Solving the Jigsaw Puzzle That Is Your Life) launches I'm also launching The Rise Above Summit, which is a spin off from The Rise Above Show, and also launching the ***BLISS** Retreat for Women*!

**B**elieve in Yourself

**L**ove Yourself

**I**dentify what is holding you back

**S**et free what no longer serves you

**S**et course on achievement of even your biggest dreams & goals

And will be as the owner of Ultimate Achievement Books will be having authors contributing chapters to the Rise Above Challenges Anthology Book Series with a compilation of Authors who serve in each of the 8 Dimensions of Life.

*I everything I create and share with my entire platform is with the purpose and intent to make life changing results!*

So, Now let's begin with your puzzle...Are You Ready?

# CHAPTER 1

❧

# Dream Weaving Through Achieving

*"When I'm drawing up a business plan, I try not to overcomplicate it. If it can't fit on the back of an envelope, it isn't worth the paper it's written on. One of the most useful things I do is to draw up two columns, with the positives on one side and the negatives on the other. It's very simplified, but it works."*

—Richard Branson

The University of Scranton shared a study from the Inc. com website which showed only eight percent of people achieve their yearly goals. How? How can it be that a mere eight percent achieve what they set out to accomplish and a staggering ninety-two percent don't?

Being a person of research, I became determined to find out what those eight percent are doing from start to finish to achieve their desired goals. I believed this was more important than trying to figure out the reason why ninety-two percent don't.

To do this, I broke it down into pieces and came up with the idea of how I could teach people to learn to be *Living Outside the Box while they Learn to Break the Cycles of Limiting Beliefs and Design Their Destiny and live their lives to their Fullest Potential.*

Our puzzle box comes with many different pieces. Some boxes may have 250 pieces while others have 1,000+ pieces. Even our pictures will end up being completely unique.

Using the jigsaw puzzle analogy, I started working on not only how the eight percent are achieving their goals, but also creating a system for people of any age to work on their own jigsaw puzzle. By using this system, they will have a framework available to follow when they are ready. The entire platform is based on helping people who read this book and/or participate in any webinars, trainings, events, or membership programs to be able to grow their Soft Skills.

Top 10 Soft Skills:

- Strong work ethic
- Dependability
- Positive attitude
- Self-motivation
- Team orientated
- Organization
- Working well under pressure
- Effective communication
- Flexibility
- Confidence

One common theme among the eight percent was they went back to the basics. As Richard Branson often says, "Keep it simple." From this point, I decided to create a system so anyone could achieve his or her goals. By breaking everything down into simple formats, people can go from weaving dreams to achieving them.

We all come with fully loaded software to achieve anything we set our minds to; we just need to read the manual of how to operate our thinking/achieving process. First, you need to believe in something. There has to be something that or someone who drives you to rise each morning and continue your journey. This is your WHY, which we'll cover a bit later in this book.

You must also be curious, courageous, and consistent. Are you the kind of person who always makes the best of a situation, or do you cry "Why me?" all the time? The journey of putting your jigsaw puzzle together begins with a commitment to yourself that you're going to get started. Most people don't necessarily fail in life; they just fail to get started.

It's time to set high goals, dream big, and put your plans into action. Yes, I promise life will happen, but having your goals/dreams written out with a plan for achieving them will keep you focused. There will be times when you fall behind going after your goals, but you can always pick up where you left off and your 3 Ring Binder will right be there for you.

Once the commitment has been made, find a comfortable space where you can quiet your mind. Take a deep breath and slowly release it. Concentrate on your goal.

Envision what the result of achieving this goal will be like. Author Stephen R. Covey said, "Start with the end in mind."

During the process of weaving dreams to achieving them, there will be obstacles which will confront us. These obstacles will prevent us from being effective and successful if we let them. It's our baggage, so let's name and claim it!

Your biggest piece of baggage is fear. Some say fear is False Evidence Appearing Real or False Expectations Appearing Real, but perhaps it should be Face Everything And Rise. Once you confront your fear, the fear goes away.

As an example, I had a fear of putting my thoughts out there to be judged and belittled. As a woman, there aren't many of us yet who stand up for our worth. I honestly have the belief that this book and entire platform has the possibility of making positive changes in this world, allowing for a better life for my grandchildren and future generations. Giving everyone a more positive view out their own Belief Windows.

I was battling fear of failure when it came to get this book out there. One fear was the acceptance from others, especially authors, readers, and publishers. Would they like it? Would they believe in it? I also had a fear of not getting it written, not getting it published, and not having any sales.

And there was a fear of never seeing my book in a bookstore or library.

I also had a goal/dream of speaking from the stage and making a difference in people's lives, but there was also a fear of how to make that happen, seeing this field was dominated by men and I'm a woman, very new to the scene.

Then another fear hit me. It was a great fear. What will happen if my entire platform becomes a success and makes a positive difference in people's lives all over the world? Tony Robbins was correct when he said, "Stop being afraid of what could go wrong and start getting excited about what could go right."

Along with my great fear was what would happen if I didn't step up, work through my fears, and achieve my dreams and goals, utilizing the system that I know for a fact works if you follow it, I know this because I always have used this system myself!

Guess what? Once I put it all on paper, the greatest fear won! I faced my fears and they vanished.

**As you begin doing your assignments at the end of each chapter be sure to place your answers and**

**information into your 3 Ring Binder under the proper tabs.**

*REMEMBER with Change comes Opportunity and I promise that you will end up finding more opportunities on your journey to Goal Achievement!*

Below, list three fears you are currently dealing with:

_____

_____

_____

Now list the positive or opposite things of these fears that you listed above:

_____

_____

_____

## Binder Assignments and Checklist for Chapter 1

☐ Think of how your life is a jigsaw puzzle and determine what phase of the puzzle you are currently at or working on.

☐ Are you being curious, courageous, and consistent?

☐ What do you see out your Belief Window? Are they FEARS?

☐ List three fears you're currently dealing with. After each one, do your best to explain why you think you have that fear. Next, write down what it would look like, feel like, and be like if you didn't have that fear. These are your opposite, positive fears.

☐ Start thinking about your WHY. What is it that motivates you? Dig emotionally deep for why you want to accomplish this. What difference will it make to or for your life? What difference will it make in others' lives if you accomplish your goal? What reward will you have?

☐ *Remember to put anything in the parking lot if you are not ready for that piece yet, date it and check the parking lot every Planning Day!

# CHAPTER TWO

ℰ

## The Weaving Process Begins

*"Be daring and choose to be different, even if it's*
*unpopular. Thinking uniquely will lead to*
*exceptional outcomes, while doing things as others*
*do will result in more of the same. Defy the norm, be*
*curious, and don't accept the status quo."*

—Jonathan Alpert, psychotherapist, executive coach,
author of *Be Fearless: Change Your Life in*
*28 Days*

Have you given any thought about what your jigsaw puzzle will look like when it is complete? We've already started the process by turning some of the pieces over to make them easier for you to identify, so now let's move forward and turn over the rest.

What is your current goal/dream? Do you have it written down? Have you constructed a plan for reaching your goal/dream? Gretchen Rubin, author of *The Happiness Project*, says, "Goals such as 'eat more healthfully,' 'exercise more,' or 'get more fun out of life' are vague. Make it clear to yourself what you're expecting from yourself. Goals such as 'bring my lunch to work every day,' 'take a 20-minute walk after work,' or 'make a lunch date with a friend every Friday' are easy to measure." In other words, your goal(s) should be to the point.

As you write down your goal(s), be as specific as possible and include a deadline(s). While it's great to have a few goals, you should **limit yourself to no more than three to concentrate on at a time.** *If you do have more than one that you are going to be working toward, be sure that they complement each other and will coincide with the end picture that you visualize.* Trying to focus on more than three goals at a time will make the process entirely too difficult if not impossible. People don't realize that they only have enough in their reserve (time, energy, and money) to spend on one to three goals that coincide at a time. For most people trying to do too much will lead to self-sabotage.

Imagine tapping into that one reserve of your willpower and inner-self and using it all at once on multiple goals such as dieting, exercising, personal growth, family, friends, work, and finances. How long before you stop dieting and exercising? How much personal growth are you going to gain? Where do your family and friends end up in the process? Do your work and finances begin to suffer? It's easy to get overloaded and lose focus as sometimes working through a system with one goal is challenging enough.

Writing down your goals and coming up with a plan for achieving them will prevent overload and improve your concentration. One of the best outlines for writing down your goals is the S.M.A.R.T. (Systematic, Measurable, Action-based, Realistic and Relative, and Time-based) plan. Taking it a step further, I encourage people to use a S.M.A.R.T.E.R. plan which includes Editable and Revisable. More on the S.M.A.R.T.E.R. plan in the next chapter.

Tackling one task in a single area of your life and pouring everything into it creates the momentum needed to continue. After you've mastered that goal, move on to the next one. *However, it is possible to work toward multiple goals if they coincide and flow together to create the intended result.* If you choose to chase more than one goal at a time, be specific with scheduling and budgets (time, energy, money) for each part of your plan.

### Now, let's DREAM!

Find a quiet space, one that is comfortable to you. Relax, take a deep breath, and let it out slowly. While doing this, concentrate on your goal. For some people this is much easier said than done. I'm the type of person who can't sit still and simply relax. If I look around the room, I notice certain things need to be done or attended to. In addition to that, I'm the one who always puts other people's needs, wants, and desires ahead of my own.

If you're that type of person, I've written a letter specifically for you. This may plant some seeds for your dreams and open your Belief Window to your new possibilities.

<u>Dear Friend,</u>

*You may not be a religious person, so my spiritual self is saying this prayer for you as well as for myself today. "Have a willingness in your life to open doors and allow yourself to absorb personal power that you can attain by fulfilling your hunger for knowledge and learning, new direction in your life, and to achievement. To do this you will need to allow yourself to find a way to Clean/Clear your Desk/Plate/Mind and begin to live your Journey, whatever it may be, wherever it may be, with not only intention, but also with action!"*

One of my favorite and inspiring quotes which I relate to dreaming is from author Joey Reiman (*The Story of Purposes*). He says, "Some ideas are bigger than others, and the Master Idea—your purpose—is the biggest of them all."

What is your purpose? Is it a dream or goal concerning family or career? Is it getting healthy or making a difference in the world? What is your burning desire?

One of our first and last loves in life should be self-love. We learn to judge others by their actions and judge ourselves by intentions. One of my goals in writing this book is to help people realize that our purpose in life is not to get ahead of other people, but in fact get ahead of ourselves.

I'm a grandmother that doesn't just knit, I cliché…meaning that I have found the secret of power found in other people's wisdom / old adages!

Remember, you have software which you are born with—you can achieve anything if you set your mind to it. When it comes to working on and achieving your goals, the best advice is the old adage of "How do you eat an elephant? One bite at a time." Break your goals down into manageable tasks; don't try to reach your goal in one day. If your goal is to lose fifty pounds, you'll never achieve that in a single day. By setting up various tasks you can do daily, however, it's possible to release that weight in a healthy way over the course of four or five months.

When I look back at where I was and realize where I am today, I'm amazed I waited so long to share this system which has worked so well for me on several occasions. I had a bunch of notes and a huge dream of writing a book to share my system with as many people as possible. If I could use this system and change my life, why can't others?

The truth is: they couldn't until I wrote my book. It's not that anything I teach, or share is new, it's just hopefully the way that I'm bringing it to you to connect to. Writing this book, I had to take all that I had learned here and there over the years and figure out how I wanted to lay it all out to make sense to people. Once I broke the pieces down to eat that elephant and wrote my goal down using the S.M.A.R.T.E.R. plan, not only did I achieve my goal of writing my book, but now I've added other products and services to my platform. This allows me to be able to earn my living working when I want and from wherever I want.

Let me tell you, my life wasn't always like this. Far from it. I've always known that if I ever wanted anything in life that I had to work for it. It was drilled into me that if it was worth having it was worth working for. For the biggest part of my adult years I was a self-employed business owner, a licensed cosmetologist and registered massage practitioner, who owned and operated a full-service salon, having my own private label of skin care and cosmetics. It was a huge challenge, toiling away for sixty to eighty hours every week to cover overhead, all other expenses, and put some money into savings. I also worked in the corporate world for many years for fortune 500 companies. In one position I was responsible for overseeing 400 women, in the other it was in retail. While in the corporate world, I endured long periods of time away from my family, numerous business meetings, and many long hours at the office. During all of these hours, day in and day out, whether being self-employed or in the corporate environment, I was able to raise a child (primarily as a single mom), purchase a home and vehicles, take vacations, enjoy a social life, and get married four times and divorced three. But while in the corporate world, I did meet my soul mate who is now my fourth and forever husband. I had to kiss a lot of toads to find this prince. My personal life will be at least a couple other chapters for my memoir.

I wouldn't have been able to do any of that if I didn't dare to dream, learn how to set S.M.A.R.T.E.R. goals, create plans and work through them, and always be curious, courageous, and consistent. I was fifty-one when I decided that the next chapter of my life was going to look a lot different than the first fifty years, because I was now ready to share what I've learned the hard way.

I had invested thousands of hours, lots of money, and effort over the years into books, courses, and seminars related to personal, professional, and financial growth. I gained much knowledge and it has all paid off. With this book and business platform, my goal is to take everything that I have learned and break it down into bite able chunks (eating the elephant) to help anyone from middle school to the age of retirement achieve any S.M.A.R.T.E.R. goal they set for themselves.

My jigsaw puzzle by the age of fifty-one had proven my theory—we won't know what our final picture will look like since it is quite a collage. Part of my collage was discovering a writing workshop. One of the presenters at the event "promised" to show me how I could write a book, and then by using their "repeatable system" I could create a best-selling book and build a business model around it. Although skeptical of their claims, I was ready for the challenge of digging deep inside myself to discover just what it was that I was meant to share with this world.

I didn't have to dig too deep. My first passion is to help women who are single parents as I was one myself for many years; I want them to be able to carve out a better life for themselves and their children. The more research I did, the more I found out what I had in my heart and mind to share. It was not just limited to women and children, but I learned men could benefit from it as well. I found that the platform I was planning to launch would be beneficial to people of all ages, sexes, colors, races, and denominations. Research also showed my concept would help people in college choice, career choice, getting into the workforce, and turning the page to start a new chapter after retirement.

Still, getting this book written the first time, then writing the second edition, as well as launching and relaunching my platform was a struggle. It was breaking down walls, bursting through limiting beliefs, and accepting that not everyone understood my passion. Many people from my inner circle maybe did not truly understand what I was attempting to accomplish. Therefore, they could not support me in the ways that I needed. Family and friends did not totally understand my passion for the project and commitment to my vision. They tried to tell me that maybe I shouldn't pursue that goal, or maybe I should change it to be less than what I envisioned. When I confronted my nay-sayers and put my consulting, coaching, and conquering skills to work, everything really kicked in.

I started working with some key folks and laid some groundwork for my Peer-to-Peer Mentoring and Accountability Membership Program, My Community, as well as my Empowerment Network & Mastermind Group. From the momentum gained from that, I said to myself— Game On! And I hit the ground running.

Then, the publishing company that I went through to publish and print the first edition of my book, ended up closing their doors and going out of business. They broke the two-year contract that they had with me and many others. Putting me in the position of having to shift gears and get everything done all over again. It was like the White Snake Song, "Here I go Again on My Own".

Those words powered me to prove to myself once more that this is still meant to be the start of an amazing journey!

Then came the Global Pandemic of the Coronavirus / Covid19. Do you think I let this stand in my way? NO, is the answer, I just had to edit and revise my plans, and get busy working with the pivots needed to make the adjustments!

That is when I dug deep and got more serious about my show. It morphed from "Keep Focused on Your Future", to "The Patricia Jo Grover Show" where we turn Believers into Achievers, then to "The Rise Above Show" with Patricia Jo Grover where we Rise Above our Challenges and Turn Believers into Achievers...and guess what I'm going to to going & growing!!!

When do you want to get started on your amazing journey? As the old saying goes, "If not now, when?"

Ask yourself this honest question: "What is holding me back?"

It is now time to identify potential obstacles. Is it certain people in your life? Is it the lack of education or a certain skill set? Or is it fear(s) as we discussed in Chapter One?

In the space below, write down what or who is holding you back. Be sure to record all your findings in your 3 Ring Binder

.

_____

Make a list of people or connections you may NEED and why you NEED them. List what additional knowledge and skills you may NEED or may be NEED to hire out. By upgrading your knowledge and skills, you will have the empowerment to achieve.

Achieving any one of your dreams or goals can be a huge transformation. Let's continue your journey by doing this exercise: let your mind loose. Allow yourself to get crazy ideas, be creative, and for this moment be fearless. Think... What if these things—money, time, physical limitations, energy—were no issue? What would it feel like, smell like, taste like? What color, flavor, and size would it be? There is no right or wrong answer; just dream and imagine it.

It must come from within you; no one else can do it for you. Someone telling you what they want for you, like a parent, a teacher, or a loved one won't work. If the vision of your goal or dream doesn't take root in your heart, it never will become YOURS.

Allow me to be the one who cares and believes in you, maybe even more than you do yourself. Open your Belief Window to the fact that you are worthy. I want to see you set one goal which is to have at least one goal or dream identified and written down by the time you finish this chapter. Remember, you can have more than one, but no more than three. If you have two or three, they must all be able to blend cohesively to get you to your one end result.

Here's an example: Diet and Exercise = Lose Weight = Healthier. It's not lose weight or get healthy. That's too vague. It's short and to the point. Diet being one goal and exercise being a second goal gives you the result you envision, which is being healthier.

When it comes to achieving goals successfully, you need to be aware of what can negatively affect your progress. Do any of the words below describe what you do? Or are you the opposite? Think about how each may affect what you are trying to achieve. I call this list Thought Starters, as it's designed to get you thinking. There is a binder assignment at the end of this chapter using Thought Starters.

## Thought Starters

**Procrastination** – There's nothing more stressful than having something weigh on you until the very last minute, followed by the panic of not being certain you can get it done. If you want to make an easy job seem hard and make sure you don't do it as well as you could, keep putting it off. Procrastination is the top form of self-sabotage.

**Clutter** – Clutter derives from the English word clot, and it clots our ability to function well. When you tolerate clutter, you're allowing yesterday's junk to interfere with your ability to reach what you need in the present. Find simplicity and order and you'll find opportunities for growth.

**Negativity** – Negativity is an incredibly destructive force that can come from many places and/or people. Being in a world where we're barraged with negative information, it's easy to be lured in. But giving negativity a place gives it power. Make it a habit to focus on the positive side of things. You may not be able to change events, but with a positive mindset you can change perceptions and outcomes.

**Comparisons** – It's in our nature to look at what others have or do and see how we measure up. But it's a pointless exercise, since there will always be someone with more and someone with less. It distracts you from the only comparison that's valid—between yourself and your goals. Stop comparing and find your strength. Think about any racer—auto, bicycle, car, runner. Is it better to be in second place for most of the race because it keeps you focused and gives you that little extra to keep up and push on? Or is it better to be the one up front, always looking behind to see if someone is creeping up on you? Will being up front cause you to slow your pace or push you harder so others don't pass you as you are running out of fumes?

**Perfectionism** – Anyone who's suffered from perfectionism knows it doesn't necessarily make you better and often leads to disappointment or failure. Focus on doing what you do well with excellence, which is much more motivating than perfectionism.

**Dishonesty** – To tolerate dishonesty—from others or from yourself—is one of the most stressful things you can do to yourself. Lies may seem to smooth things out in the moment, but ultimately, they do nothing but create complications and anxiety.

**Mediocrity** – Everyone wants to feel they measure up to standards in general. Think about whose standards you are using for yourself. Have you established any of your own? Tolerating mediocrity from yourself leaves no room for greatness. When mediocrity is accepted, excellence, uniqueness, and true success die. Aspire to excellence, always. Revisit Comparisons! Think of the quote by Norman Vincent Peale, "Shoot for the moon. Even if you miss, you'll land among the stars."

**Guilt** – Guilt weighs us down and crushes us. It's tremendously stressful whether it's deserved or not. Guilt never truly accelerates us toward what we want. Make your choices and live with them. You may regret some things; if so, make adjustments and don't repeat. Take note and learn the lesson from the mistake, but don't allow guilt to take hold.

**Excuses** – Excuses may come in handy when you don't want to do something, but they also keep you from doing the things that you are meant to do. If it's important, then you will have to find a way to make it happen. Excuses have never once moved anyone closer to their goals.

**Enmity** – The essence of enmity is insecurity (low self-esteem, negative self-image), which manifests itself as discontent with ourselves, and that causes great stress. If we allow this to take root, we react to others in hostility and anger as an automatic defense mechanism. We then alienate others and separate ourselves from our own potential. Enmity comes from clinging to negative experiences, so choose to move on instead of hanging back in anger. To have a better future, you must be heading in that direction. It's like driving a car; to get where you are going, 99.9 percent of the time you need to be looking out of the windshield, not the rearview mirror.

**Rejection** – We often interpret rejection as ourselves not being good enough, but that may not be the way that it was directed at us at all. When we receive any form of rejection, it's bound to create stress. What I'd like for you to do is think back to any rejection you have ever experienced. What was your first reaction? Did you automatically conform with that reaction? If so, how did it turn out? From this point on, with ANY rejection you get, allow yourself to take a moment before ANY reaction. Take a breath and realize that it is NOT a personal attack. There can be an array of reasons, some of which may have nothing to do with you. So, assign each new rejection a number associated with its importance. If it is a high priority, put it back on a To Do list; if not, move on and continue! Like failure, rejection is often a necessary step to the pursuit of success. If you've never been rejected, your goals probably aren't ambitious enough or your dreams big enough.

**Defeat** – How stressful it is to feel defeated with something associated with your life. It is possible to experience failure without defeat. Everyone fails at some point, but instead of being defeated and allowing your failures to define who you are, use them as a guide to learn and better yourself and improve your odds of success next time.

**Binder Assignments and Checklist for Chapter 2:**

☐ Write down your current goal(s)/dream(s) and attach a deadline(s) to them. Insert this in your binder, making it the first page. Goal Sheet(s).

☐ Find a quiet space and get focused on your goal and take a look out your Belief Window. Is it beginning to change?

☐ Define what's holding you back. (Graveyard Tab = threats/ weaknesses)

☐ Create a list of people, connections, knowledge, skill sets needed. (NEEDS List)

☐ Start thinking about applying the S.M.A.R.T.E.R. plan to your goal(s).

☐ Add updates or notes to your purpose and your WHY under your WHY tab. We will develop your WHY in the next chapter.

☐ Under your Toolbox tab, create two headings. On the Strengths sheet, list what is working for you and under the Opportunities sheet, list what is available to you. These can be your current skills, your will, your connections, and your positive responses to your Thought Starters list.

☐ Under your Graveyard tab, create two headings. On the Weaknesses sheet, list what you feel are your current weaknesses. Under the Threats sheet, list who or what may be holding you back from achieving your goal. These can be skills you need to grow, your lack of will or desire to follow through, lack of connections, and your negative responses to your Thought Starters list. Be sure to review your Fear tab, as that list may have some of your weaknesses and threats. The Graveyard tab is where dreams go to die, so we don't want things to get piled up too far and get buried. With our planning sessions we start shoveling through them and planting the seeds to make them grow into something useful for our toolbox. The stuff on that list that we can't change for the positive we don't need any more, so bury it and move on.

☐ Update any or all sections of your binder where necessary and you know there's been growth or change, no matter how big or small. Under the Parking Lot tab, write down any questions, ideas, or comments that may not have been covered yet. You should do this daily to start.

☐ Start to think about what your mantra or creed is going to be. We'll cover this in the next chapter.

Remember this will be going on the back of your

3 Ring Binder in the clear sleeve.

•*Remember to put anything in the parking lot if you are not ready for that piece yet, date it and check the parking lot every Planning Day!

# CHAPTER THREE

### 𝆕

## Defining Your WHY

## and

## Developing your Sensory Vision

*"When God puts a dream or a promise on the inside of you, he deposits within you everything you need to accomplish it."*

—Joel Osteen

It's now time to define your WHY and focus on creating your Sensory Vision. Having a strong WHY is important because it's the catalyst which will serve as your motivation.

Your WHY…Whether you call it your purpose, mission, vision, ultimate goal, or by any other name your desire is an absolutely vital ingredient to your success. So vital, in fact without it (or I should say, without enough of it, anyone can have a little desire), even following my system to the letter will not get you the results that you want. On the other hand, if you do have the yearning desire, there is no way that using it as the tool it was designed to be cannot work!

This is your "WHY", invest as much time and effort as you need to in order to see, feel, smell, taste, touch, and hear it. Then revisit it as OFTEN as necessary. Learn to develop your Sensory Vision!

Seek specific help. An excellent way to get the support that you may need is to find a mentor or coach that has already prospered using the system.

Let you mentor take you by the hand and show you the way. Ask for constant feedback- and utilize it!

You will cut your learning curve dramatically and realize the fruits of your labor in a lot less time. When working to achieve your goal(s) there will be times when the energy just isn't there or the distractions become too loud. That is when you want to revisit your WHY. It will reenergize you and deafen the distractions.

To determine your WHY, you need to discover if your WHY is a want, need, or desire. This will take a lot of inner soul searching. By taking the time and energy to do this, you'll end up not only answering if your WHY is a want, need, or desire; you'll realize just how strong it is. This process can be very emotional, but it's also a great reward. Your WHY may be related to your personal wellbeing, either emotional, spiritual, physical, or financial. Take the time necessary to drill down and discover the real reason behind your WHY. It may even turn out that your WHY is completely different than you originally thought.

Once your WHY begins to take shape, so does your vision. Every time you close your eyes, you'll start to envision your puzzle—complete! Sometimes this will seem so life-like. You will start to feel it, see it, smell it, taste it, hear it, and most importantly, you'll believe in it. Have some fun with this step.

Your WHY needs to be actionable with language that resonates with you. Here's an example of how a strong WHY works.

Imagine an Olympic athlete in training. She wakes up at 5 a.m. every day to exercise, commits to a strict diet, and signs up with a coach or trainer who pushes her beyond her limits. She is not doing this for fun; she's doing it for her WHY. Her WHY is to come in first place and win the gold medal. She pictures herself on the platform, holding up her country's flag and having her picture taken for the whole world to see. Her WHY supplies her with the motivation needed to achieve that goal.

Why is it so important that you achieve this dream or goal? Who, or What is it that motivates you? Why do you get out of bed every day and work so hard to move forward towards achieving you goal? What is the reason that your mind gets filled with the thoughts that you just have to do this?

Write down three things that will motivate you on a daily basis. (This could even be part of the fears you listed in Chapter One). There certainly should be a lot more than three, but for now list the first three that come to mind. Remember to dig emotionally deep for why you want to accomplish this.

What difference will it make to or for your life when you achieve this goal? What difference will it make in others' lives if you accomplish your goal? What reward will you have?

1. _____

_____

2. _____

_____

3. _____

_____

Your vision is built upon the foundation of your WHY once you've determined it and should be in sync with your WHY. As you work toward your goal(s) or dream(s), picture in your mind the exact outcome. Sometimes the best way to bring your vision to life is to close your eyes and see it. Imagine having already achieved your goal. Use all your senses, like "VISION", this doesn't mean actual sight.

I want you to think of it more like a creative imagination. So creative that if you dream, or even just close your eyes in a peaceful setting that you can See yourself having Achieved that dream or goal.

I'm going to encourage you to go OVERBOARD with your imagination. To not only be able to Envision/See it, but to... hear it, smell it, taste it, and FEEL It (physically & emotionally)!

Work on this to create a Sensory OVERLOAD! To the point you may physically get goosebumps, smile, or tear up! Have it become as real as possible in your mind!

Now, use your creativity and search for anything and everything that can show representation to you of those thoughts, feelings, sites, smells, tastes, etc.

AND put them in front of yourself on a daily basis.

Create a VISION BOARD or Collage, by finding pictures that come as close to you Having Achieved the Result that you want. You can even create a Vision Board for each milestone you are having to accomplish along the way like steppingstones to reaching your goal. It may help to put dates on these pictures to help keep you motivated seeing those dates everyday as you look at the pictures!

You may find these pictures in magazines, online, or maybe even in your own photo album, and find short motivational phrases, pasting them to a board as you go.

Once you get the VISUAL piece of the puzzle put together keep it and copies of it in places that you see on a daily basis.

This could be on your bathroom mirror, the dash of your car, on your desk, on your Screen of your Computer, or phone, on your refrigerator, and my personal favorite is in the *front sleeve of your 3-ring binder.*

*Now that you have the VISUAL PIECE of the puzzle locked down, now let's plug in the other senses that I had recommended. Be creative with this piece of the puzzle!*

Really use your imagination here...........................

So, for example...If you goal is to purchase a home on some Tropical Island and be living there full time... Then the Sensory Vision of ACHIEVEMENT of your goal may be to be sitting on the beach just out your backdoor as part of your celebration of achieving your goal, Then I suggest to surround yourself with the things that will stimulate your senses.

Close your eyes and take a deep breath and let it out slowly...................................................................
........................................................................
........, has this started to plant some seeds for you?

For the SMELLS this could be a car scent, a room atomizer, a candle, even linen spray for your bed.

The TASTES could be Cocktails, Fruits, Candies, Chewing Gums, etc.

The SOUNDS could be beach waves and seagull meditation music, it could be your alarm music, or even the ring tone on your phone, etc.

And for the FEEL you could have a Zen Sand Garden on your desk, some kinetic sand, and even a little foot wash bucket of sand to stick your bare feet into and wiggle your toes. The Feel can also be the Emotional Feeling that you have connected to your Goal Achievement!

You may even want to go as far as to schedule yourself some tanning appointments!

**So, my friend do you now understand the assignment that I'm giving you is to not only figure out your WHY, and Create YOUR Total Sensory Vision,**

**but how important it is to begin with your WHY as the foundation.**

## Mantra

According to Dictionary.com, a mantra is "an often-repeated word, formula, or phrase, often a truism." It is well documented that the Beatles, long before the world knew them, had their own mantra. Whenever a band member was feeling doubtful about becoming successful, John Lennon would ask, "Where are we going, fellas?" to which the other three would respond, "To the toppermost of the poppermost!" Then Lennon would say, "Right!" This mantra of theirs fueled them with the needed motivation to continue with their music and chase their dream of becoming one of the world's most successful rock 'n' roll bands of all time.

As you think about what your mantra will be, try to tie it into what your goal or dream is all about. This is something that you should commit to your memory and repeat often.

I personally went through the alphabet and wrote down three positive words to go after "I am". I recommend checking out EmsPath.com for their Affirmation / Mantra Guides they are created for Manifestations (health, wealth, confidence, etc.). We work more on your mantra in the binder assignments at the end of this chapter, but for now jot down any ideas about what your mantra might include in the space below.

_____

_____

_____

_____

_____

It's also important to set aside ten to fifteen minutes per day to concentrate on your goal(s) and your WHY. This is not the time to be working on them; this is time to envision the outcome, I personally suggest meditation. Feel yourself having achieved the goal. Your WHY was the reason(s) for achieving the goal. Keep in mind that your goal(s) can be broken down into long-term, medium-term, and short-term.

So, concentrate or meditate on your goal or the part of the goal you're currently working on.

## The S.M.A.R.T.E.R. Plan

If you've attended business meetings, seminars, or network groups, you've probably come across what is referred to as the S.M.A.R.T. plan for setting and achieving goals. It's an acronym which stands for Systematic, Measurable, Action-based, Realistic and Relative, and Time-based. While there are books written about this, here it is in a nutshell.

**Systematic** – Your goal should be broken down to the smallest steps possible and prioritized.

**Measurable** – You must be able to track your progress whether daily, weekly, monthly, quarterly, or yearly. Celebrate your milestones and revise your goal, as necessary. Remember to revisit your Graveyard, Toolbox, Notebook, and Mantra.
Also, be sure to add to your Planner or Calendar as well.

**Achievable / Action-based** – The most important step in achieving a goal is to take action. Be mindful of your limits, but, stretch yourself at least a little. Pushing yourself just a bit can create great results and move you forward.

**Realistic and Relative** – You want to be able to meet your goal and achieve that feeling of success. If it's easy, it's not worth it. Remember, eat that elephant one bite at a time and make sure each piece has meat on the bones.

**Time-based** – Every stage of the process of achieving the goal in its entirety needs to have a time limit attached to it. Since each stage is a piece of the puzzle, all stages will need to be completed by an end date. It always needs to be a realistic time frame; remember that you can't lose fifty pounds in one day. When working through this process, make sure under your Planner or Calendar tab to transfer things from your Calendar into your "Design Your Own Destiny Planning System". Make this part of your daily routine and use your Planning System to set up reminders and view deadlines. In the information that I share in my "Design Your Own Destiny Planning System" I talk about Parkinson's Law…this law is regarding time management and productivity. "Work expands so as to fill in the time available for its completion."

So, taking Parkinson's Law into consideration while planning & scheduling if you schedule something to take 20 hours it will take 20 hours. If you schedule it to take 10 hours, it will.

I have added an E and R to the S.M.A.R.T. plan, which is Editable and Revisable. These things need to be planned for and put into the equation for the purposes of Murphy's Law, human nature, and the simple fact that life happens. These pieces of your puzzle are key. Here they are:

**Editable** – Tracking your progress through calendar management and charting, and tracking your budgets of time, energy, and finances is important. You need to be aware of how each part of the process is being used and that it is on target with your short-term, medium-term, and long-term goals. Edit your time, energy, and finances when and where necessary.

**Revisable** – Once the Measurable step is complete, determine if it needs to be revised, even just slightly. Occasionally a wrench gets thrown into the works and messes with your game plan and budgets (time, energy, money), therefore your goals must be Revisable.

## Self-evaluation

While the big picture is important, make sure you don't get overwhelmed and lose focus. Look at your pieces (binder) and know where you are currently. Have a clear picture and then give yourself an honest self-evaluation. In the spaces below, you will write down what you need to

Learn, Believe, Need to Have, and Do. This will be added to your binder once you reach the end of the chapter. It's helpful to have your calendar page from your binder and your actual calendar in front of you for this exercise. As you go through each step, write down tentative deadlines for each.

What do you NEED to Learn? Is it a software program? Is it people management skills? Is it a new system for tracking your progress? Write down what you NEED to LEARN.

_____

_____

_____

What do you NEED to believe in to achieve your goal(s)? Is it a higher power (God, Christ, Infinite Intelligence)? Is it acceptance? Is it perhaps yourself? Write down what you NEED to BELIEVE in.

_____

_____

---

What is it you NEED to do when it comes to achieving your goal(s)? Do you NEED to take a class and learn a new skill? Is there someone you NEED to call or send an email to so you can connect with them? Write down what you NEED to DO.

---

\

---

\

---

What do you NEED to have? Is it more time or finances? Do you NEED assistance with your short-, mid-, or long-term goal(s)? Is it certain material or equipment? Write down what you NEED to HAVE.

---

\

---

\

---

Once these steps have been completed and all your notebooks have been re-visited, you should have a truly clear picture of where you are currently. This gives you your Starting Point "A" that gets plugged into your GPS. Now we start putting the puzzle pieces together to build on the foundation that you have just laid.

These re-evaluations are meant to keep you from straying too far off track and to keep you focused on making progress toward your goal.

## The Could Have, Should Have, and Would Have Syndrome

How many times has something happened so fast or unexpectedly in your everyday life and you were not tuned in because you were on autopilot? We will never be able to avoid slipping into that mode, but we can make choices so that we seldom experience regrets for things that we have done. Always remember that your conscience will be your compass. As we put our puzzle pieces together, let's try not to have any that are labeled Could Have, Should Have, or Would Have.

Time truly is the wisest counselor in many ways. Always remember nature, time, and patience are the three greatest physicians. Be sure to take moments where you can step back, draw in a deep breath, revisit your past, calm your mind and soul, and experience some of nature's amazing beauty.

The best profit for the future comes from the past. None of us would be the person we are today if we hadn't lived through what just happened yesterday, let alone our entire life. This is true for every single one of us on the planet. We could even break that down to the hour, minute, or even second in some cases. No matter how we break it down, we can find all the wonderful, good, bad, and ugly that has happened in our lives. It is how we process, deal, cope with, and ultimately learn from the past that defines our future. It is these things, events, and feelings which we turn into the building blocks of our life.

We learn in different ways, but one thing all creatures and humans alike share is that our past guides us. Some learn the hard way, yet there are those who learn to use their past to shape their future. Here is another place that our Belief Windows play a big part in our lives journey.

Knowledge helps you make a living, but wisdom helps you make a life.

People make mistakes when they don't take the time to look back. I certainly know I learned this lesson the hard way. I'm not suggesting you go back and find things to regret or be pulled backward, but to move forward in a healthy direction requires a look in the rearview mirror as well as the windshield.

I'm sure you've heard the saying that luck is what happens when preparation meets opportunity. If you are under-prepared for anything that is important to achieving your goals, chances are you will say it was bad luck. Although I can't recall who said this, it's etched in my memory for eternity: "Poor planning leads to poor performance." Over the years it has proven true time and time again for many people.

The odds of reaching your goals dramatically increase when you set plans to achieve them. Know that you will always encounter adversity but realize that overcoming it is prosperity for greatness.

When setting your plans to achieve your goal(s), think of planning a trip using a map. Your goal is to get from point A to point B. The map covers many miles and there are roadblocks, potholes, detours, and some roads may be closed. So, you need to carefully outline your travels so you can get from point A to B, avoiding as many obstacles as you can. Use this map approach when planning out your goal(s). Think ahead, look ahead, and take the road with the fewest bumps along the way.

## Binder Assignments and Checklist for Chapter 3:

☐ Start your motivational list under your Toolbox Tab.

☐ Define your WHY, which is the first tab in your binder, per goal. Remember, your WHY must be actionable and use language that resonates with you. It needs to be motivating! Dig in deep for this. Look to your Emotional Why!

☐ Create a complete Sensory Vision & Vision Board. Find pictures, smells, tastes, sounds, and feels that inspire and motivate you.

☐ Create your mantra. Once you have a mantra that works, write it down on the Who Am I? page, which is in the sleeve on the back of your binder. This way it's always a simple glance away when you need to read it.

☐ Apply the S.M.A.R.T.E.R. plan to at least one goal by doing the breakdown in the Notes tab for that section.

☐ Conduct your self-evaluation. Be incredibly open and honest with yourself during this exercise. Have you started seeing differently out of your Belief Window yet?

☐ Think of your goal(s) using the S.M.A.R.T.E.R. map system and add your findings into the places that correspond (Calendar, Learn, Do, etc.).

*Remember to put anything in the parking lot if you are not ready for that piece yet, date it and check the parking lot every Planning Day!

# CHAPTER FOUR

෩

# Pack Your TRUNK for Your Journey!

*"Success is the sum of small efforts—repeated day in and day out."*

—Robert Collier

Think of the last vacation you took. Did you travel to a resort on a tropical island or was it a ski trip to Colorado where you took to the slopes? Regardless of the destination, you packed a suitcase (or two) with what you needed. Depending on where you were headed, it was sandals versus ski boots and Bahama shorts versus a winter jacket. It's also good to always expect the unexpected because that is just how life goes.

While life may not always be a vacation, it is certainly a journey. And when you're taking a life journey, you need to pack your trunk.

Things to include in your trunk for the journey should be your WHY, your vision, your mantra, and your binder. Once again, I'm going to refer to the old adage, "How do you eat an elephant? One bite at a time." This adage is relevant in business, sports, writing, and your life. It is a proven method for reaching a goal or dream.

It is better to enjoy your journey through life, and you do this by putting yourself first. A day of worry is more exhausting than a week of hard work. Alleviate the worry by breaking down the things which appear too large to cope with all at one time. It's a bit of extra effort up front that separates the winner from the people in second and third place. When it comes to goal achievement, doing something, taking action, making the first step is what gets results. Talking about it doesn't.

People tend to get wrapped up and busy with things that don't really matter. It's easy to get consumed by what is happening around you; think of social media. It makes it difficult sometimes to stay focused on your goals. It's good to work hard, but you've got to learn how to play hard, too. It's a balancing act. I once heard somebody say, "It's not that life is so short; it's that we wait so long to begin living." If we want to genuinely enjoy our journey of life, we must make the time to stop and smell the roses. Do you appreciate the people you love? Do you hug your children before you leave each day and give your spouse a kiss? When was the last time you called your parents to tell them how much you love them?

If you make it part of your S.M.A.R.T.E.R. plan and stay committed to enjoy your journey of life, you'll live with no regrets. You'll see your plan for achieving your goals working in front of you. In the end, you'll be able to say, "I made the most of my life. I enjoyed my family. I enjoyed my friends. I achieved my goals and finished my puzzle with joy." Let's jump right in and pack your trunk!

**Binder Assignments and Checklist for Chapter 4:**

☐ From your binder, take out your two Journey Elephant sheets, A and B. On the first elephant "A," in the trunk area, write #1 Self (learn to put yourself FIRST), #2 Health, which will include physical, mental/spiritual, and financial (How you make your income. Then pay self-first=retirement fund emergency fund, vacation fund, miscellaneous fund), and #3 Loved Ones, which includes family, friends, and pets. These are always your top priorities and will come first over anything else.

☐ In the stomach area of the elephant write down Fear Of, and then list failure, what ifs and buts, and lack of time (or money, skill, will, confidence, self-esteem, or support system). Fill in all the pieces that are still on your mind. These will be second in priority.

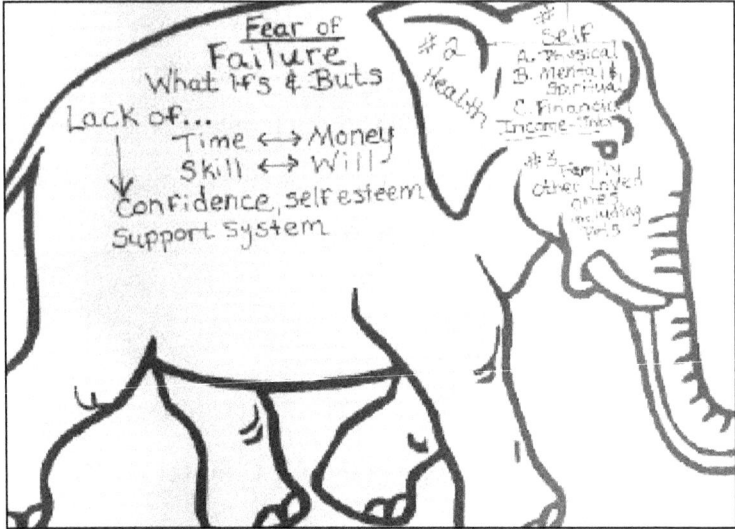

☐ Now take out your second Journey Elephant "B." In the stomach area write down Everyday BAGGAGE. This is where we name it and claim it! These are things in our lives and home that may get in the way at some point. This can be unfinished business and/or other people's needs (wants, desires, sickness, schedules). These relate to anyone not in your home but who you may be responsible for.

Once you have your two Journey Elephants complete, is there anything that should get packed into the trunk for your journey? Are there certain things you've learned in this exercise you need to keep at the top of your mind? Is there anything that may affect your day-to-day life if not addressed?

Get the information you have learned into your 3-Ring Binder under the proper tabs, and date it!

• *Remember to put anything in the parking lot if you are not ready for that piece yet, date it and check the parking lot every Planning                              Day!

# CHAPTER 5

❧

# Benefits of the S.M.A.R.T.E.R. Plan

*"Our goals can only be reached through a vehicle of a plan, in which we must fervently believe, and upon which we must vigorously act. There is no other route to success."*

—Pablo Picasso

Now that the framework of your puzzle is complete, it's time to start building. This is where you get to put the pieces into place and fit them together. It's planning to live your life—your way—which means you need to accept all of your actions, good and bad. A majority of people feel like they're adrift in this world. They work hard but don't seem to get anywhere, the old expression of two steps forward, one step back.

A key reason for this is they haven't spent enough time thinking about what they want from life. If you were to ask fifty people at random, "What do you want from life?" most would likely say, "I don't know" or "I never thought about it." They haven't set formal goals. Would you set out on a major journey with no real idea of your destination? Probably not!

The binder that you've been building is your road map. The S.M.A.R.T.E.R. plan is your navigation system with all the bells and whistles. Keep in mind, no matter how good or up to date your navigation system is, it won't calculate for the unexpected detours, construction, accidents, traffic, rest stops, or pulling over for an important phone call. But if your S.M.A.R.T.E.R. plan is filled in, it will provide the best route to reaching your goal.

Here is an example using the S.M.A.R.T.E.R. plan. In this scenario, you want to increase attendance for a webinar you're hosting.

**S.M.A.R.T.E.R. Plan Goal:** By April 10, the day of the webinar, I want to see a 15 percent increase in sign-ups through my social media.

**Specific:** Through Facebook messenger, Twitter, an email campaign, and blog posting, I want to increase the number of sign-ups for my April 10 webinar.

**Measurable:** A 15 percent increase is my goal.

**Achievable / Action-based:** Last webinar saw a 10 percent increase in sign-ups when promoted only through Facebook.

**Realistic / Relative:** When my webinar generates more leads, my sales team will have more opportunities to close sales.

**Time-based:** Deadline is April 10, four months for promoting.

**Editable:** I can do heavy promotion or paid ads on Facebook or switch to posting more blogs. Once I measure which format is getting more results, I can concentrate more effort on that media outlet.

**Revisable:** I can change my percentage mark, advertising outlets, and even extend the webinar date.

It is important to put in the effort of creating your S.M.A.R.T.E.R. plan. As we discussed earlier in this book, sometimes our puzzle gets pushed aside or we don't work diligently on it. Life does happen and things can and will sneak up on you. It's OK to add time to your journey if necessary or adjust your budget (time, energy, money), but it's not OK to give up. That is why you should review your WHY and look at your vision board on a daily basis. Zig Ziglar once said, "People often say that motivation doesn't last. Well, neither does bathing – that's why we recommend it daily."

When you're putting the pieces of your S.M.A.R.T.E.R. plan together, be sure to answer or include the following:

**Specific:** Be truly clear. Try answering the five "W" questions: What do I want to accomplish? Why is the goal important? Who is involved? Where is it located? Which resources or limits are involved?

**Measurable:** A measurable goal is one that you can track your progress in and stay motivated. Be sure to include: How much? How many? How will I know when it is accomplished?

**Achievable / Action-based:** Your goal needs to be realistic and attainable. How can I accomplish this? How realistic is the goal?

**Realistic and Relative:** This is about ensuring your goal has value to you. For your goal to be relevant, you must be able to answer "yes" to the following questions: Does this seem worthwhile? Is this the right time? Does this match my other efforts or needs? Am I the right person to reach this goal?

**Time-based:** Your goal should have a target date. When? What can I do six months from now? What can I do six weeks from now? What can I do today?

**Editable:** Track your progress for short-term, medium-term, and long-term goals. Does anything in your goal need to be edited? Do all the components coincide?

**Revisable:** Once the Measurable step is complete, determine if it needs to be revised. Do you need to tweak any of the budgets (time, energy, money)? Does the whole plan need to be broken down further or revised in any area?

Let's slip into the past just for a moment. Remember what I said in Chapter Three: people make mistakes when they never take the time to look back. Moving forward in a healthy direction requires a look in the rearview mirror as well as a look through the windshield. Take a moment to think of each success and failure you've had. They can be huge successes and major failures or a small milestone and just missing the mark. Either way, review them in your mind. We'll revisit this in our binder assignments at the end of this chapter.

**Binder Assignment and Checklist for Chapter 5:**

☐ Review your goal(s) and make sure you've applied the S.M.A.R.T.E.R. plan. Fill in each part completely and honestly. This will be your navigation to the achievement of your goal(s).

☐ Make notes under all the tabs required. List each success and failure you thought of earlier in this chapter. Break each one down to pinpoint the good points and the bad points. How can you use these? What did you learn? Write it down and be sure to date each entry.

☐ Make a commitment to yourself to work toward your goal(s) on a daily basis. Start a schedule of daily, weekly, monthly, quarterly, and yearly reviews. Write it in your Planner or Calendar tab and transfer it from your Calendar to your "Design Your Destiny Planning System".

☐ *Remember to put anything in the parking lot if you are not ready for that piece yet, date it and check the parking lot every Planning Day!

# CHAPTER 6

## 🐚

# Never Give Up!

*"Doubts are contagious. Fortunately, confidence is equally contagious."*

—Patricia (Patti) Jo Grover

Self-doubt is simply lack of confidence. It's bound to happen at times when you're piecing your puzzle together. Its questions racing through your mind like, "Is this good enough?" "Can I do this?" and "Is it worth it?" A lot of this comes from your Belief Window and was placed in your mind as young as childhood.

Let's address that last question, "Is it worth it?" The direct answer is, yes, of course it is. If your goal wasn't, you wouldn't have written it down or applied it using the S.M.A.R.T.E.R. plan. You probably wouldn't get out of bed every morning if it wasn't worth it. That is why I amended to the S.M.A.R.T. method, the E and R (Editable and Revisable). When self-doubt rears its ugly head, you can edit or revise your goal, regain your confidence, and continue putting your puzzle pieces into place.

It's time now to give your inner critic (negative self-talk and self-doubt) a name. Better yet, we're going to give it a face and personality. Think of a bad, notorious, ruthless character. What does s/he look like? What does his or her voice sound like? What about this inner critic makes him or her so bad?

Next, draw a picture of what s/he looks like. Don't worry if you're not an artist; you will not be graded on this assignment. When you look at the picture, who is it? Is your inner critic a Hannibal Lector, Pennywise the clown, or a wicked witch? After you name it, hang it. Put it in a place where you'll see it often. As you pass by it make at a face at it. Tell it using a strong voice how you have confidence in your goal(s) and in yourself.

By naming and challenging that inner critic voice, you are taming it. You weren't born doubting yourself. Those voices are not who you are at the core. They like to hide and

sneak up on you when you are vulnerable. Tame them by saying, "Not this time. I know you and your game." Remind them, and yourself, of times when you've overcome tough circumstances. They will take a step back.

Also beware of critics who are telling you that failure is on the way. Whether these people are intentionally trying to push you off course, misguidedly trying to keep you from getting hurt, projecting their fears onto you, or just jealous that your success might challenge them to do better, they are not people you want to rely on.

Doubts are contagious. Fortunately, confidence is equally contagious. As your Belief Window changes you can begin to see a brighter future. You can find positive, successful people to hang out with in the Peer-To-Peer Mentoring and Accountability Membership Program, and my Empowerment Network & Mastermind Group offered through my website at www.PatriciaJoGrover.com.

I think author Cheryl Strayed said it best: "It's up to you to make your life. Take what you have and stack it up like a tower of teetering blocks. Build your dream around that." That is what your binder and this book is all about. It's laying the foundation, fitting the pieces together, and creating your life—the complete picture on the box. But in order to arrive at your goal(s), you need to silence the self-doubt.

These are some ways you can turn down the volume of your inner critic.

**Treat Yourself Kindly** – Put yourself first, especially when it comes to your health (refer to your Journey Elephant #1). We find it easier to be compassionate toward others rather than to ourselves. Take a step back and imagine that someone else was in the situation in which you are criticizing yourself for. Would you be hard on that person? Probably not. Try applying the same standards to yourself.

**Permission to Ask** – The truth will set you free! Ask yourself, "What's the worst that could happen?" Perhaps the worst outcome of any goal is the world as we know it comes to an end. What would happen if you were kicked out of the family or your country? How about being cut off from family or friends? While this may be disappointing and possibly embarrassing, so what? It's more likely the image in your mind is much worse than the reality.

Don't forget to ask yourself the opposite, "What's the best outcome that could happen?" Keep your focus on your vision and end goal. By focusing on the goal and the little successes, you will get to the goal. So, give yourself permission to ask away!

**Talk to Someone** – Whether a professional or a good friend, sit and chat about what's on your mind. What fear are you trying to overcome? Sometimes a simple conversation

and just hearing your situation spoken out loud can make a world of difference. Again, I'll mention our Peer-To-Peer Mentoring and Accountability Membership Program & Community offered through my website at www.PatriciaJoGrover.com.

**Keep a Journal** – This is a great way to sort through emotions as well as challenges. Pick up a journal and write freely whatever is on your mind. You can brainstorm, write a poem, or just write down random thoughts. What is unique about this process is it is easy to revisit what you were thinking and feeling at that time. From there you can analyze it, draw conclusions, and quickly get through that emotion or situation should it reappear.

Self-doubt is quite common. It does NOT predict failure. The only failure is not taking action. Even if there is failure, it is only temporary. The first step in working through fear and doubt is to have a success, no matter how small. Fear and doubt will diminish, and more success awaits. Some people work on smaller goals first to gain inner-strength and grow their self-esteem before tackling their bigger goal(s). If you don't take control over your self-doubts, they will have control over you. As your Belief Window changes so will your overall outlook on life!

In my position as a consultant, coach, Conquering Skills educator, and mentor, I have found that many people find life is already tough enough without having to deal with being overwhelmed and filled with self-doubt and fear. Here's the good news - this is 100 percent fixable!

With the right mindset and applying the strategies I've outlined in this book; anyone can move from a state of overwhelmed and fearful to a state of success. Make sure all of your self-talk is positive and that you're keeping your Belief Window bright and shiny!

**Binder Assignments and Checklist for Chapter 6:**

☐　In your binder, go to your Graveyard tab and work on your inner critic voice. Break down what the voice is saying and replace it with positive affirmations. Get some of these things moved off this list!

☐   Name and draw a picture of your inner critic. Hang it on the wall. Be sure to let him/her know who's in charge and why.

☐   Review and follow the ways to silence your inner critic, Polish & Shine that Belief Window!

☐   Check out the Peer-To-Peer Mentoring and Accountability Program, and Empowerment Network & Mastermind Group at www.PatriciaJoGrover. com.

☐   *Remember to put anything in the parking lot if you are not ready for that piece yet, date it and check the parking lot every Planning Day!

# CHAPTER 7

### ૬ৡ

# Understanding Failure

*"Most people hate to fail, and for good reason—failure is no fun. But those who perform best do so by building up their weaknesses rather than ignoring them.*

*A foundation of success is accountability.*

*Take ownership of your failures. Question, learn, and acknowledge them, and then use that process to eliminate weaknesses and become better at what you do."*

—Adam Bornstein,

*New York Times* best-selling author and founder of "Born Fitness"

There are two rules when it comes to failure:

1. It is OK to fail.

2. Understand the failure.

The first rule is hard for people to accept, but it's necessary in order to move forward and achieve your goal(s). Failure is just a step toward success. As an example, look at Thomas Edison, a genius, inventor, and public figure. It is well documented that he failed more than a thousand times when trying to get the incandescent light bulb to work. Imagine if he quit after the first failure, or the tenth, or even the one hundredth. You'd probably be reading this book by candlelight.

Stories of successful people knowing that failure is OK are innumerable. Think of someone you consider to be successful, regardless of their occupation or field of expertise, and do some research on them. I guarantee you'll find they experienced a failure or two on the way to success. Winston Churchill said it best: "Success is going from failure to failure without losing enthusiasm."

The second rule can be a tough one to accept. Most people accept their failure but never understand it. It's important to understand the failure, meaning look for the lesson that's there. Break the failure down and ask what happened and why. Referring back to Thomas Edison and his lightbulb,

when asked about all the failures, he said they weren't failures; he simply learned a thousand ways in which it didn't work.

Let's redefine failure. First, it is proof that we are actively pursuing something (a goal) and not sitting around waiting for something to hopefully fall into our lap. Secondly, it provides us with feedback of what did not work and what did. Celebrate what worked and change what did not. Often, failure is unexpected successes in disguise.

Failure is something that we've all experienced in some form, big or small. The size of the failure is irrelevant; it's your reaction to the failure that is important. Yes, failure can burn, it can sting, and it can hurt, but only if you let it. It's imperative you discover the lesson within the failure, grow from it, and continue toward your goal.

Think for a moment of the clichés that go side-by-side with failure. Any time you've failed or someone you know has, what do you hear? "Look on the bright side" or "Learn from your mistakes" and "It'll only get better from here." We've all heard those phrases, but what purpose do they serve? They all have a hint of truth in them and are meant to inspire us to continue toward the goal. Through proper planning, you're less likely to worry about being judged for what others know should have been done differently. It is only human nature to make mistakes and then redeem yourself, hence so many rags to riches stories.

Keep in mind that there are more people rooting for you than you probably think, people who admire you for your curiosity, courageousness, and consistency. It may be uncomfortable and scary to share your failures, but you are not the only person in the world to have failed.

Imagine if the results of failure were something we could physically see. What would the pain and disappointment do to you outwardly as it does internally? The purpose of this explanation is not to say you may fail miserably as much as it is to say you have the ability to make it not overwhelming, scary, and uncomfortable.

This is why I advise you add to your Planner or Calendar tab daily, weekly, monthly, quarterly, and yearly. It will make you take accountability for your failures, so you learn and grow from them. We are all human and we all will experience failure(s) at some point in time. But now you know how to understand the failure and fit that piece into your puzzle.

## Habits

Let's start with an example. It's Friday night and your friends call you and say, "Hey, we're all going bowling and then out for pizza. Want to join us?" It may have been five years since you last went bowling, but you're all for hanging out and catching up with your friends, so you accept the invite. After getting your shoes, picking out a ball, and finding which lane you're assigned to, you enjoy a few games of knocking down pins and praying for a strike every time. The next morning when you wake up you realize that your entire body hurts. How did that happen? You didn't fall and land on your arm, you didn't bang your arm, and no one punched you in the arm either. Why then does it hurt? Because you used muscles while bowling that you don't use on a daily basis. Those muscles weren't accustomed to that workout. Now, the person who bowls on a league every Monday and Wednesday after work has conditioned those muscles for the movements associated with bowling. It's the same concept when it comes to habits.

Habits we create through routine behaviors that we repeat on a regular basis. They more or less become an unconscious act and a fixed way of thinking or doing something. To us our own habits often go unnoticed because most of the time we don't need to engage is self-analysis. But in the case of digging deep to create our Actionable Plans of Goal Achievement we must do so.

Good news is that your old habits may not be bad ones, and if they are, they are hard to break, but not entirely impossible!

Everyone has habits, some good, some bad, and some ugly. Creating positive and effective habits is critical to success in your personal and professional life, and the only way to break bad habits. We hear about all kinds of different habits that we should have from eating, sleeping, exercising, etc. Thought leaders and motivational speakers regularly reinforce the importance of creating good habits. More importantly, it's not creating the good habit; it's making it stick. Look at the typical New Year's resolution—going to the gym. You start out all gung-ho, going three times a week, and then life starts to happen. You miss one workout, then another, and all of a sudden, it's been two months since you hit the gym, so you cancel your membership.

So how do you make a good habit stick? The Live Bold & Bloom website has broken it down into seven changes you should make.

1. Start ridiculously small. Don't try to completely develop a new habit overnight.

2. Get hooked on your habit. Make sure you find something about the new habit which interests you.

3. Have clear intentions. Instead of "I'll try," start saying, "I will."

4. Celebrate your small wins. Set milestones both big and small…. I say to Budget (time, money, and energy) for these planned celebrations.

5. Design your environment. If your habit is to eat healthy, don't have junk food in your house.

6. Surround yourself with supporters. Spend time with like-minded people and those who have already developed the good habit you want.

7. Pre-commit to your habit. Always envision yourself doing/living with the good habit.

I say all good habits need to have prioritizing and sequencing. Organization is key. My Design Your Destiny Planning System will help you create the new healthy habits that you are looking to form. With easy steps of A, B, C's & 1,2,3's. Remember the road map exercise; things are easier when planned ahead.

Prioritizing – What is the most important? Time, energy, money?

Sequencing – What needs to be done first, second, and third?

As you begin to prioritize and sequence your new habits, certain steps of the process will fall into one of the following categories:

- Don't want to do but need to do

- Want to do and need to do

- Want to do but don't need to do

- Don't want to do and don't need to do

Look at each step necessary for you to establish a good new habit and ask yourself which category it fits into.

A great resource for doing this is……... *Eat That Frog! 21 Great Ways to Stop Procrastinating and Get More Done in Less Time* by Brian Tracy. There is also a workbook which accompanies this title.

I've recently become acquainted with another woman author from Maine, Kim Smith. Kim and her husband, Ryan both had an incredible weight loss journey that they were on together. With Kim's first book Unbelievable Freedom is where they share that story that transformed their health and happiness with Intermittent Fasting. One of the other books she has written is titled "Poster Girl Habits" Creating an Intentional Contentment Practice. This book is about her 5 Habits that if you develop and layer these habits it supports your flow of contentment.

Habit One- Energy

Habit Two- Expectation

Habit Three- Easy Delights

Habit Four- Everyday Rituals

Habit Five- Editing

**Boy does any of this sound familiar to what I've been sharing with you through this book?!**

Kim & Ryan have other books that she and others have written under the umbrella of Unbelievable Freedom Books.

**Binder Assignments and Checklist for Chapter 7:**

☐ Think of a past failure and break it down. What was the lesson? What good came from the failure? Write it down under your Notes tab.

☐ Begin to develop at least one good new habit. Prioritize and sequence it.

☐ Under your Graveyard tab, look at your bad habits and start taking action to change them.

☐ Check out *Eat That Frog!* by Brian Tracy.

• *Remember to put anything in the parking lot if you are not ready for that piece yet, date it and check the parking lot every Planning                           Day!

# CHAPTER 8

❧

## Staying Focused

*"Stay true to yourself, yet always be open to learn.
Work hard, and never give up on your dreams, even when
nobody else believes they can come true but you. These are
not clichés but real tools you need no matter what you do in
life to stay focused*

*on your path."*

—Phillip Sweet

Congratulations! You're making great progress with your puzzle. Your Belief Window is staying unfrogged. All your pieces are turned over and you've started to fit them together, so let's stay focused and keep going.

Have you ever been at work, looked at the clock and it was 10:30, then in what seemed like the blink of an eye it was 12:30 and time for lunch? Where did the time go? How did it get to be lunch time already? Well, time certainly didn't change. A minute is still sixty seconds, and sixty minutes is still an hour. The reason time went by so fast was you were so focused on the task in front of you.

No one interrupted you. Your boss didn't come into your cubicle and neither did any co-workers. Your phone didn't ring, no customers came in, and you were able to drown out the noise of the copy machine. Simply put, you had no distractions.

Distractions can be a double-edged sword. You can't completely avoid them, and they can be either an intrusion or a blessing, the difference between your neighbor's dog continually barking while you're trying to sleep with the window open versus a pleasant phone call from an old friend wanting to catch up.

## Discovering Discovery

The process of discovery can be an odd thing. It can happen at any time, although it's usually the result of hard work and study over a period of time. In many cases it's deliberate, but sometimes you uncover things very unexpectedly.

People can spend years working toward a particular goal or engaging in research that finally yields the proper conclusion, whether or not it is what they had originally expected. However, discovery can be accidental. Hard work and research are still involved, but in this situation that eureka moment may have come more or less out of the blue with something new.

The story behind 3M sticky notes is that they were trying to create an adhesive that would be permanent. With every attempt there was a bit of failure. Finally, after breaking down the failure, they came up with the idea of a reusable adhesive applied to a small piece of paper. They took the positive lesson from the failure and created a success.

## Keeping Distractions Under Control

Distractions are altogether different from discoveries. They are exactly what they sound like—things that take our attention away from the task at hand and redirect it elsewhere. Granted, many good ideas came from a distraction, but for the most part they're intrusive and pestering. Certain distractions can only be ignored for a short while, such as a leaky faucet dripping or a yard that needs mowing.

Considering the sheer number of distractions that appear throughout our day, not to mention that they appear while we're hard at work on something else, the vast majority of these ideas can and should be put off until later. Any distraction which is a non-emergency should be added under your Parking Lot tab. This will allow you to continue your progress with your nose to the grindstone but not completely forget what the distraction wants you to do. There's more on this in your binder assignment at the end of this chapter.

Now instead of eating our elephant one bite at a time, we're going to address the elephant in the room. When it comes to distractions, by far the biggest of them all is social media. It's connected to us 24/7. It's on our laptop when we log on, it's notifications to our phone, and it's even in our daily conversations: "Did you see what she posted on Facebook?" or "Did you read what the president just tweeted?" The world of social media is extremely easy to get lost in, and it's responsible for many lost hours.

How many times have you logged onto the internet to look something up and "bing," there's a notification from Twitter or Facebook or "you got mail" tells you an email has arrived? Then next thing you know you're scrolling through Facebook "liking" and "hearting" pictures, or checking out Twitter, and end up reading a blog post or two. Then you navigate over to your email and start to delete junk email, advertisements, and maybe respond to your friend or co-worker. Remember our example about time going by so fast earlier? That's what happens when we enter the world of social media. Time gets away.

While I don't suggest you give up social media, I certainly suggest that you control it. The same way you would limit your child to only a couple of hours in front of the TV or playing video games, you need to limit your social media time.

Many leaders have scheduled time in which they go through their email, and they even set up their spam folders to catch certain emails, so they don't clog up their inboxes. Some people use the auto response for emails, which notifies the sender that they only check their emails at certain times during the day. This will likely be a challenge to start, but once you develop this habit, you'll gain more time—more productive time!

Also, try setting or scheduling a couple of hours to concentrate on a certain task and turn your phone off or at least put it in silent mode. Phones now-a-days are a huge distraction. They are attached at our hip and constantly vibrate and ping every hour, sometimes even more often. Another suggestion would be going into your phone settings and scheduling your push notifications. Instead of your phone pinging every time there are Facebook or Twitter updates and an email coming through, it will download all your notifications at scheduled times, like every hour or two hours. It's a great way to curb the distractions but still not miss anything.

This is not to say we should allow ourselves to fall into a rut—far from it. Once you've committed to a goal, give it your best attitude and commit to the work and time for it to come to fruition. You can't do that if you're constantly jumping from idea to idea, leaving a host of unfinished activities in your wake. Give your ideas and projects the time and energy they deserve and let them reveal to you which ones are discoveries, and which are merely distractions.

At times, discoveries can seem similar to distractions and can be easily confused. Despite their similarities, they are drastically different. It is only by understanding the differences that we can move forward working on our jigsaw puzzle. Otherwise, we'll spend too much time on tasks that subtract from our long-term success rather than adding to it. You owe it to yourself and your future to stay focused!

**Binder Assignments and Checklist for Chapter 8:**

☐ Review your Planner or Calendar tab. What needs to be added? What have you already accomplished? Have you transferred things into your "Design Your Destiny Planning System"?

☐  Schedule your social media time. Put a notepad and pencil next to your computer and jot down the time you log onto Facebook or any social media site. You'll be surprised how much time you actually spend there. Look for apps that can block your social media for a scheduled time.

☐  Create a distraction list under your Parking Lot tab. Later, you can evaluate, prioritize, and explore each one. Should they be a part of your goal? Are they a future goal? Are they worth your budget (time, energy, money)?

☐  *Remember to put anything in the parking lot if you are not ready for that piece yet, date it and check the parking lot every Planning Day!

# CHAPTER 9

&

# Articulate, Activate, and Achieve!

*"The love of what you do, combined with your belief in
what you do, will not determine your
success. It will determine how hard you will work
and how dedicated you will be to achieving it. Success just
shows up from there."*

—Jeffrey Gitomer

It's time to really home in on your goal(s). You've done a lot of work since Chapter One. Your goal is written down, your WHY has been discovered, a vision board has been made to bring your goal into sight, your mantra is keeping you motivated, and you've been building a fantastic binder for use now and for future goals.

There are two kinds of people in this world—winners and those who have not yet learned how to win. Having your binder complete, you are a winner. Any time you feel you're struggling or self-doubting, review your binder— every section of it. That's what winners do!

It's time now to complete the puzzle!

## Articulate

Our next step is to articulate your goal. What does it mean to articulate your goal? The word in itself has a few meanings, but let's use it as a verb, as in *to articulate an idea*, meaning to give clarity and distinction to.

By applying the S.W.O.T. Analysis and the S.M.A.R.T.E.R. plan to your goal, you've done just that. You became clear on the intention of your goal, broke it down into manageable pieces, and have been moving forward in achieving the goal. So, let's keep going!

Start scheduling a bit of time every Sunday to review and plan for the upcoming week. Revisit your binder, reread your goal(s), make adjustments under any tab where needed, and make a task list. It's good to include things which pertain to your goal as well as other tasks (distractions) which may need your attention. It has been proven that people who make a list accomplish more than those who don't.

There are a few steps involved when it comes to articulating your goal. In a nutshell they are:

- Time – Spend time reviewing your goal. This should be done daily.

- Atmosphere – You need to create an inspiring atmosphere when working on your goal or in your binder. It may be burning a candle of a certain scent, listening to music, or being outdoors.

- Brainstorm – When ideas or distractions hit, jot them down, preferably under your Notes tab in your binder.

- Take Breaks – Set up a break pattern for yourself. Every hour or so, take ten minutes. Stretch, go for a short walk, or step outside for some fresh air.

- Review – Go over your S.M.A.R.T.E.R. plan, your mantra, and your binder. Sometimes by looking something over twice, a new idea or angle may come to you.

- Commitment – Reread your WHY. It will empower the commitment you made for this goal.

- Accountable – Hold yourself accountable or get a partner to hold you accountable. Again, you can check

  out my website www.patriciajogrover.com for the Peer-to-Peer Mentoring and Accountability Membership Program and Community.

- Peers – Who are you spending time with? It's important to spend time around like-minded people. Stay away from the negative nay-sayers.

- Positiveness – Stay positive, focused, and don't give up.

- Celebrate – Be sure to reward yourself for lessons learned, milestones (big and small), and new discoveries. *Be sure to ADD Celebration into your Budget of Time, Money, and Energy to reward yourself for your progress when you achieve milestones along the way, as well as when you Achieve your Goal!*

## Activate

Activate is easy. You activated your goal even before you decided to purchase this book. Your goal was wrestling around in your mind and the noise grew so loud you needed to do something. You made the choice to get serious about obtaining your goal and found this book. That is what I mean by you already activated your goal.

To activate simply means to set forth in motion or to turn on. In relation to your jigsaw puzzle, it's turning over the pieces, fitting them together, and having the big picture on the outside of the box come into focus. Every time you're adding and working in or on your binder, you're activating your goal. Each exercise in this book is part of the activation process. Let's face it; if you sit around waiting for your goal to be reached, it will never happen.

What are some other ways you've activated your goal(s)?

_____

_____

_____

There are four basic steps to activate your goal:

1. Have a clear intention on what your goal is. This is why we used the S.M.A.R.T.E.R. plan and created our WHY and mantra.

2. Homework is necessary. Spend time researching your goal or certain aspects of your goal. Keep learning, and as Stephen Covey wrote, "Begin with the end in mind." In other words, know what your picture is on the outside of your puzzle box.

3. Understand failure and find the lessons within each one. Break the failure down, study it, learn from it, tweak it, and move forward.

4. Take action all the time, even if it's baby steps. Each movement forward brings you closer to achieving your goal.

And, of course, plan to win!

## Achieve

This is what it's all about—finally reaching your goal. Achievement can mean many different things to all sorts of people. It's how one measures success. For some it's fame and others it's fortune, and some claim it's both. Still others say it's time with family or being a part of something which is bigger than them, like starting a foundation or organization for those less fortunate. The sad part is some people reach their goal and then grow despondent and depressed. This is because they no longer have a WHY or a goal to work toward. If you start to feel this way, review your distraction list. There could be a new goal hidden in there for you.

How do you define achievement and success?

_____

_____

_____

As you start to approach the final step(s) toward your goal and complete your puzzle, take a moment, and review all you've done so far. In the beginning you had a goal in mind, and you're about to complete it, reach it, see it, etc.

Take a brief moment to celebrate (watch your favorite movie, have some ice cream, take in a ball game, paint, read) and then do your binder assignments.

**Binder Assignments and Checklist for Chapter 9:**

☐ Visit www.patriciajogrover.com and check out some of the *FREE RESOURCES* I have there for you. Then check out my 1:1 Consulting, Coaching, Mentoring and my Peer-to-Peer Mentoring & Accountability Membership Program and Community.

☐ Start to schedule Sunday planning time each week. You should also do monthly, quarterly, and yearly planning sessions for your larger/long-term goals. Be sure to refer to your Planning or Calendar tab, and transfer into your Design Your Destiny Planning System.

☐ Continually articulate your goal(s) and use your binder during the process.

☐ Continually activate your goal until you achieve it.

☐ Define achievement / success and write it down under your Notes tab.

• *Remember to put anything in the parking lot if you are not ready for that piece yet, date it and check the parking lot every Planning Day!

# CHAPTER 10

&

# Life Outside the Box

*"The major reason for setting a goal is for what it makes of*
*you to accomplish it.*
*What it makes of you will always be the far greater value*
*than what you get."*

—Jim Rohn

Congratulations!

All your pieces were scattered as you dumped them out of the box, and by going through this process (book) you've fitted them together to create your puzzle (binder). It's time now to live outside of your puzzle box! And enjoy the view out of your new Belief Window! Your future is bright!

Always refer to your binder as you go through life. Set new goals and use the process you now know. Be a winner, or if necessary, reteach yourself to be a winner.

## Living Outside the Box,

### *The Goal Achievement Strategist's Guide To Reaching Your Full Potential and* The Design Your Destiny Planning System

Are the tools we use to help you to be

### *Solving the Jigsaw Puzzle that is Your Life*

Now that you're living outside of your puzzle box; the box you had put yourself in or had allowed someone else to put you in. Dare to dream. Always have a vision and set S.M.A.R.T.E.R. goals (short-, medium-, and long-term). Be sure to Articulate, Activate, and Achieve anything you set your mind to. Define your Who, What, Why, Where, When, and How. Plan, schedule, and track your budgets (time, energy, and money) for each. Be curious, courageous, and consistent all the way through the process.

Create an actionable winning game plan for achievement based on strategy, careful planning, positive mindset, determination, focus, flexibility, and the fundamental concepts you learned in this book.

That is what living outside of your puzzle box is all about: Achieving!

## The 3 Cs

The three C's of my business are Consulting, Coaching, and Conquering Skills Education. Let's review each...

**Consulting** – This is where we dig deep to find out what you genuinely want as a result. We develop a clear picture of what's in your mind. During an hour phone call, we review your dream, set goals, understand the S.M.A.R.T.E.R. plan, and begin to carve a path to achieve them. You'll need to have your ideas ready, notebook and pencil in hand, and have a calendar. We will conclude with a set date and time in which you will have your vision (pertaining to your goal) ready.

**Coaching** – Once we have your picture, we next determine what your obstacles/threats, strengths, weaknesses, and opportunities are. Then we determine how to navigate, repurpose, leverage, and utilize our findings while creating your S.M.A.R.T.E.R. plan. As we work further, I guide you to develop your concept or plan through a series of conversations.

**Conquering** – This is where you put your plan into motion—activate. Start thinking about who you want on your team. It's where you realize the importance of focus, determination, and flexibility. There will be ups and downs, so you need to keep your positive attitude. I will continue to motivate, support, and guide you as you work through any issues that arise.

The benefits of the three C's and working with me are that we discuss your concepts, ideas, thoughts, and general direction of your journey. Each session we have is personally tailored and focused on the achievement of your S.M.A.R.T.E.R. plan. We use an approach which is designed to create tremendous organization, thoughtful direction, and concentrated discussion, all focused on the end result you desire.

There will always be a wrench somewhere in the process. There will be critics and nay-sayers in life. Keep this in mind, it's not what they say about you that affects your life, it's what you say and believe about yourself that affects your life. Our Inner Critic is our own worst enemy. It sneaks up and causes self-sabotage. You need to keep your Belief Window from getting fogged up.

Having a coach who understands your mission and is there to guide you through your plan is proven to guarantee success. The wrench can be adjusted and tweaked. I will help you drown out the nay-sayers and stay the course.

So, are you ready to get started living outside of your puzzle box? It all starts TODAY!

Text GOAL to 26786 for Gifts!

Visit www.patriciajogrover. com and be sure to:

Like, Subscribe, and Follow me on all of Social Media Platforms, as you will see my title has become "Your Goal Achievement Strategist". www.PJG.VcardInfo.com

There are many articles, posts, and videos that give you FREE content regarding all things related to Goal Achievement. You will find links to all of them all on PatriciaJoGrover.com.

Attend a FREE Within One Week (WOW) prerecorded webinar and follow the steps I have laid out for you on my website.

*Good news if you have this book and have read to this point you are that much closer to being able to schedule your FREE One Hour Consultation Call with me.*

After you have completed all steps let's get you plugged into the other products and services that I provide you may need for that extra support on your journey to Goal Achievement.

Be sure now to check out the Peer-to-Peer Weekly Mentoring and Accountability Membership Program, the online courses & workshops, and Communities that I have available to you.

Thank you for letting me be a part of your journey and sharing your puzzle with me. I'm glad I was able to give you a clearer view out your Belief Window. I look forward to hearing about your successes and achievements.

**Patti@PatriciaJoGrover.com**

#Articulate/Activate/Achieve with #Curiosity/Courage/ Consistency

# ABOUT THE AUTHOR

ॐ

Patricia (Patti) Jo Grover, was born in Massachusetts and then moved to Maine, at age three, with her mother and brother to get away from a volatile situation involving her father. She will someday write a memoir, sharing the layers of what seems like many lives' experiences, not just that of one person. Through all of the struggles she learned how to still continue to move forward in life.

Patti has taken all that she has learned from her difficult childhood, and through years of business management—personal, local, and positions with fortune 500 companies—as well as business ownerships on a personal and corporate level. She has combined these together, along with her education and life experiences, in this book.

More importantly, she shows how these years and events have led to personal growth, wisdom, and the yearning to give the world a tool to help individuals to dream and even dare to set goals; to make plans, work their way through their own life puzzle, and ultimately achieve the goals and successes they desire.

Patti wrote "Living Outside the Box, *The Goal Achievement Strategist's guide to Reaching Your Full Potential*" to empower people to live their best lives possible.

Be to go to her website https://PatriciaJoGrover.com and use the social media links to like, follow, and subscribe to her other content. www.PJG.VcardInfo.com

Find out more about Patricia (Patti) Jo Grover here…Magazine Cover, and more in-depth story about life on pages 22 & 23 https://issuu.com/michelle-lemonadelegend/docs/magazine_patricia

#TheGoalAchievementStrategist, ,

#DesignYourOwnDestiny, #RiseAbovewithPatriciaJoGrover,

#ConfidenceIsEquallyAsContagious , #NeverQuitOnYourDreams

#NotStoppingNowOrEver , #BigGirlPantiesRequired

#KeepAheadOfYourself , #LiveLifeWithJoyDaily

#GetItIntoYourCalendar , #KeepFousedOnYourFuture

* 9 7 8 1 7 3 5 0 6 4 8 0 2 *